FOREST BOOKS

Route Tournante

KJELL ESPMARK was born on the 19th February 1930. He completed his doctorate in Comparative Literature in 1964 at Stockholm University and was appointed professor of Comparative Literature there in 1978. In 1981 he became a member of the Swedish Academy and in 1988, chairman of its Nobel Committee. A major poet in his own right, his first volume of poetry *Mordet på Benjamin* (The Murder of Benjamin) was published in 1956. To date he has written ten volumes of verse, four novels, seven books of literary criticism, including a two-volume study of the traditional from Baudelaire, *Att översätta själen* (Translating the Soul) in 1975, and a book on the standards of the Nobel prize in literature, *Det litterära Nobelpriset* in 1986. His poetry and his prose have been translated into many languages and he has been awarded a large number of prizes for poetry and literary criticism. Among these awards the most recent are The Gerard Bonnier Prize for poetry in 1985, The Schuck Prize (literary criticism) in 1980 and The Bellman Prize (poetry) in 1985, the last two being awarded by the Swedish Academy. A selection of his poems entitled Bela Bartock Against the Third Reich, translated by Robin Fulton, was published by Oasis Books in 1985. In 1987, a volume covering twenty-eight years of writing poetry was published by Norstedts. *När vägen vänder* (Route Tournante) was published in Stockholm in 1992, the title poem inspired by Cézanne's painting and has met with wide acclaim in his own country.

JOAN TATE has been a full-time writer, publisher's reader and translator from Scandinavian languages for over thirty-five years.

PER WÄSTBERG is one of Sweden's leading intellectuals, the author of ten novels, among them in English The Air Cage and Love's Gravity, several volumes of poetry and essays as well as books on Africa. He was President of International PEN from 1979 to 1986, Editor-in-Chief of the daily *Dagens Nyheter* in Stockholm from 1976 to 1982. He was one of the founders of Swedish Amnesty and the Swedish Anti-Apartheid Movement.

ROUTE TOURNANTE

Kjell Espmark

translated by
JOAN TATE

and introduced by
PER WÄSTBERG

FOREST BOOKS
London & Boston

PUBLISHED BY
FOREST BOOKS

20 Forest View, Chingford, London E4 7AY, UK
PO BOX 312, Lincoln Centre, MA 01773, USA

FIRST PUBLISHED
1993

Typeset in Great Britain by Fleetlines Typesetters, Southend-on-Sea
Printed in Great Britain by BPCC Wheatons Ltd, Exeter

A CIP catalogue record for this book is available from the
British Library

ISBN 1-85610-027-8

Library of Congress Catalog Card Number 93-71944

Forest Books gratefully acknowledge the financial support for
this publication from the Arts Council of Great Britain and
the Swedish Institute.

'Route Tournante' was originally published in Swedish as
När vägen vänder by Norstedts Förlag, Stockholm in 1992.

CONTENTS

Kjell Espmark

The poems contained in this book were translated over a period of about a year before the volume came out in Sweden, the manuscripts sailing back and forth across the North Sea with queries and answers to them, small changes, pleasures in finding the right rhythm, the right word, with riddles solved and solutions found, to the delight, I hope, and satisfaction of both parties – a rare privilege for a translator.

Joan Tate

FOREWORD

Per Wästberg

For many years, I have followed Kjell Espmark's writing, since 1950 when he published romantic small pieces in short-lived and youthful literary magazines.

To the world around him, Espmark shows a countenance of restraint and tolerance, wisdom and balance. No scandals have reached me, and I live in his neighbourhood and share his barber. If Dylan Thomas – to avoid naming his Swedish equivalents – had an opposite, then it would be Kjell Espmark. I would rather associate him with virtues more usually ascribed to an older poet, John Milton: diligent, moderate, learnèd and dutiful, as administratively skilful as the university rector he escaped becoming, a conscientious visitor to the museums of the world, a recluse in Gotland in the summers.

As a member of the Swedish Academy and its Nobel Committee, in an unusual way in Sweden, Espmark combines the overall look and objectivity of the scholar with the leaps through time and space of the poet. He has written a remarkable poem on the death of a drug addict in the men's lavatory at the Royal Library: thin walls separate the underworld from the tables of the learnèd.

In 'Translating the Soul' (1975), Espmark deals with European modernism as a tradition of renewal. He analyses the way modernism broke through in Sweden in 'The Soul in Images' (1977), an exemplary and advanced manual in the art of reading poetry.

Espmark's first novel is about loss of memory ('Oblivion') in recent times in Sweden, in which society functions in a promiscuous interchangeableness. The novels that followed,

'Misunderstanding' and 'Contempt', are Dantesque journeys in infernos, in which one hell is a sauna, the other a rehabilitation home. In these miniatures of awareness of problems, the reader is the main witness who is taken in and convinced by the unfortunates. His ironically matter-of-fact language starts out from bureaucratic memoes and contemporary mass media. His intention is to chart the cracks and ambiguities in society. Emotion is concealed between the lines.

Espmark's poetry appears in groups, first with epic elements in three collections between 1956 and 1961. 'The World Through the Eye of the Camera' is a significant title. Then a strictly composed trilogy, 'Late in Sweden', 1968–75: "an X-ray of society with a number of vulnerable people in focus," according to the poet himself. This concerns people who have words pressed into their mouths and whose steps are steered by external factors, not by any inner freedom. This theme recurs in Espmark's suite of novels.

The third trilogy, 1979–84 – according to the design of the poet – builds up a personal existence with love, work, and children, then continues out into Europe, where the utopia of the artist is contrasted with the reality of power – as in 'Béla Bartók against the Third Reich', the title poem in Robin Fulton's selection of Espmark's poetry (1985).

Espmark is probably the only person who has ever succeeded in making good poetry out of Swedish domestic politics. His portrait of the Minister of Finance is a classic. The secret journey of the Director for Nature Conservation is a paraphrase of Jules Verne. He is no one-track satirist; he understands the driving forces behind bigwigs as well as the impotence of the exercisers of power. He penetrates through the opaqueness of everyday life. With insidious irony, from unexpected angles, he illuminates the nooks and crannies within the façades of the welfare state.

There is a strong thematic and technical continuity in Espmark's poetry. A conversation with the past is being carried on; voices asking for life, for a listener. Against the compulsion stands the game, against annihilation the attempt to widen the preserves of freedom. What is redeeming is the word, the small gesture, the moment when "ardour and opportunity create one another".

'The Secret Meal' (1984) consists of twelve dramatic panoramas of the various empires of power. The poet is a merciless guide through history. Only eccentrics such as Mozart and Bartók refuse to submit. "I am still called Osip Mandelstam" is a poem on the victory for the man who finds a remaining word. Out of anonymity, the flicker of television and destroyed war documents, Espmark rescues a face, a cry.

Freedom is defined by the way one deals with the repetitions of history. The parallels enrich, and the clean-scraped skulls are the same above and below the earth. Friends on the way from dust to dust are those who have been eliminated from the reference books, those who have missed the main parts, erased by the intrigues of authorities, and tidied away like the scrap paper with which the cracks of time are filled. Tenderly, Espmark frees and rescues his characters from the machinery of life when it stops and takes a pause.

We are released if we glimpse our destination and start out from our tradition. Slightly guardedly hopeful, Espmark expresses this in a poem on long-distance skating:

No one is free;
each and everyone has a place in the pattern.
The tracks in the ice are there before, unyielding.
Each and everyone makes himself free.
Floating in his freedom, stride by stride,
with no contacts with the waiting tracks in the ice.
Their freedom makes the pattern visible.

Song is resistance to loss of memory. In Europe, the actual wind is a mass grave, but in a rose garden in Chartres he finds a sweet confusion of music and a NO to the doctrinal order offered by the cathedral. Espmark's Europe is Mozart's, with his sensual intelligence. In poetry, art and music, this can be captured, this "storm of forgotten faces open to nothing".

As a poet, Espmark is an anti-modernist. He does not praise the new, but seeks averted history, signs of rebellion against oppression and annihilation: "Every stone is a prisoner on hunger strike." Defiant, with no great hope, he sings them out of the kingdom of the dead: Indians, Jews, the wasted people who have been scraped off the panels of history and acknowledgement.

The dead lie hidden beneath our footsteps; their lives were misunderstanding and unredeemed demands on an inhospitable existence. History and now – the contours of a human being on the wall in Hiroshima and a young prostitute in court in New York – flow together in a flux in which the poet hears familiar voices mixed with forgotten languages.

More than anyone else in Swedish poetry, Kjell Espmark has become the spokesman and interpreter of the dead. He makes himself leader of the chorus and advocate, which is to him more essential than being an intimate subjective poet relying on the store of his own soul. His impossible dream is that every experience could be linked with another during the passing of the generations and vision merge with vision "like gleaming pieces in God's mosaic".

'Route Tournante', in Swedish 'When the Way Turns' – Espmark's latest collection, now in English – perhaps introduces a new project. As in earlier collections, it turns in the direction of history: *When a language dies/the dead die a second time.* Together with the two previous volumes of poetry, in my eyes it makes Espmark into a classic. In it are combined features which constitute his individual character: the intellectual analysis, the crystal clear sobriety necessary to *be in command of a frenzied darkness*, a symbolism of objectivity which never loses foothold in our everyday life, and a suppressed emotional intensity – a dryness which burns.

'Route Tournante' is Espmark's most personal, least guarded book. The didactic poet has gone into retreat. The great construction drawings have been replaced with drafts of what is inconceivable, the human being. Although Espmark still broadens his field of vision far beyond his own destiny, there is here a romantic pulse and a desire to let himself go.

Prague, Alexandria, Frida Kahlo Museum in Mexico are among the anchorages where he plumbs the depths and cracks and faults in his life. The least egocentric in Swedish poetry scrapes at the graffiti-covered palimpsest of history, while his own features can be glimpsed in the mirror of the traveller's room "precisely as many seconds as it takes to tie my black tie".

The one seeking her secret sister
must find the milk store
opening into the interior of the earth.

The key words are seek and find, the sister, who is what is familiar, the secret which is what is forbidden and intimate, the milk shop which is what is ordinary. The door leads downwards and inwards. If the upper surface of the earth which may be slightly frozen is scratched, in Espmark's poetry is found a seething mass of threads, roots and nourishing substrata.

His strict form is there to put disorderly objects in their place and then tip them upside-down, or with the pedantry of the scholar, to put in ranking order the chaotic elements of life so that we can more easily distinguish their connection. But when he lets Cézanne place *an angry easel in what does not yet exist*, it means that history has an away as well as an at home, in which the past and the future, the decade and the minute touch one another.

This reversed perspective makes us step out of habitual seeing and go on into *the suddenly fresh grass of last year*. The skull in the museum case sees *the time I cannot see, because I stand in the middle of it./And his eyes are large and dark with distaste*. Our actions today change what happened a hundred years ago: the passport policeman in Leningrad is the same as the Mesopotamian temple servant. Before changes place with after.

Sometimes a sudden link can arise/between times unknown to each other. In a world of false news, games of pretence and reproductions, Espmark draws on the architecture of the trustworthy and sketches rooms in which emotions, events and objects find each other. He achieves cross-fertilisations, throws out boat-hooks which draw crafts to each other as they pass in the river of history. And then there is a glimpse – as in the poem on the skaters – *a connection which refuses to give up*.

In a kick-turn of language, pessimism is repressed for a moment. The poet's self-control breaks into Mozartian cheerfulness and he brings to mind his friend Tomas Tranströmer. Intense and serious, yet treading lightly, Kjell Espmark moves from Antiquity to the Prague of Havel, from the family farm in Jämtland to the eternal present of Gotland. He seems to me to have lived very long, with undiminished sharpness of mind. And for the first time, the road is turning, cautiously but hopefully:

The meaningless has touched us . . . –
Every house is uninhabited: waiting
for whoever can make his way back.

Translated by Joan Tate

Poems

When the road turns

We are unexpectedly back in the village
among outlined houses and timeless geese
beneath sparse patches of sky:
the canvas bare between brushstrokes.

What happened?
Were we but briefly outside life?
As if a sudden butcher's knife
with four practised slices
had parted eye, throat, heart and sex
from all that is headlong on its way
through day after day to nowhere
then moved them back to a chapter
we had already been through.

All as before. Except the raging light.
As if for the first time street were street:
each scent reinforced, each colour more saturated –
the meaningless has touched us.

Madame regards us with indulgence
and serves up several bits of chèvre,
a bounteous flowering taste
dipped in ash.

Try to remember. Assume the previous
chapter still has legal force.
Recall with a thrill a rut with water,
a voice and the scent of honeysuckle
without truly remembering:
as if hurrying towards each other
with arms outspread
you find yourself hugging a stranger.

What I seek in the memory conceals itself
a monster from outer space.
Splashes of blood alone tell the tale.

But of course we have lived before?
Depends on what you mean by live.
Odd glimpses of memory tell
of a grandiose landscape
with a retroactive taste of ash.

The hotel sheets appear used:
we recognise that stain
though we have never been here before
A worn place for beginning.
Fingertips seeking your mouth
feel your lips come to life.
Tongue creating a hollow at the shoulder.
As when a scratched ritual
is visited by an unknown divinity
our love becomes
love for the first time.

I am swimming some way down
midst a twitching turning shoal.
Is it not here
the poem usually starts?
Waiting, shadows, blurred shimmer.
Suddenly I see ships up there:
an image swaying slightly,
still with many possible ends.
Two stems touch lightly.
The crews stand each in their language
spears thoughtfully raised to throw.
A youth has just fallen into the broad
turquoise band where I am swimming
with slowly petrifying strokes.
A dark brown man holding his foot
another pressing down his bubbling head.
The round enamel-still fish wait.
Century after century stiffens.

When a language dies
the dead die a second time.
The sharp word that turned the soil
in damply glimmering furrows,
the chipped word with steaming coffee,
the shiny, somewhat flaked word
momentarily reflecting
the window and the noisy elm outside,
the secretly fragrant word
a hand groping for in the dark
with timid assurances:
those words which gave the dead a life
beyond life
and the living a share in larger memory
have just been scraped out of history.

So many shadows scattering.
With no name to live in
forced into final exile.

The name of the overgrown station
is something in fifty-four letters
which none can mouth any longer.
That can be endured.
If only all those
who died for the second time
had not taken the rough of the soil along,
the green of the foliage, the cool of the brook.
Your foot may suddenly go through the ground
and no one knows what the wind wants of us
or why we once came here.
Yes, we hear the birds in the tree
but what has become of their song?

Such a persistent misunderstanding –
that Eurydice with a dying cry
should have returned to depths and darkness.
Of course, she shied from his frightened gaze –
who wants to be seen
who has been dead a week?
But reluctantly she did follow
this familiar stranger
singing her out of what was faceless
day after day after day
drowning her protests.
She lived long at his side
without living at his side.
They found it hard to grasp
how she could drink a goblet of wine
without drinking a drop
or could walk in the sun
with steps feeling their way in the dark.
Only the one she thought she loved
and sought with hesitant fingertips
appeared sometimes to understand
when he embraced yearning and air.

Sunday at Museo Frida Kahlo

After all that happened the house is closed:
a ragged communist dream
is restored in there, supervised
by the ex-lodger Trotsky.

We have procured permission to visit
but are met with suspicious wooden eye
in the hole in the green entrance:
"But you've just been in here."

We must wait while the guard seeks advice
from higher powers. A humming-bird waits with us,
a seeking flutter at rest: like time
it sucks honey from the stone itself.
Above the wall rise the leaves of world ash.

At last we are granted a repeat.
There are signs we have been here
though none of us can remember it –
tracks of my heels in sand,
our whitened names in wooden guest book,
with photographer Pappa Kahlo in his frame,
regarding us with completed face;
for several hours, his camera has
contained my averted side
only seen by his sensitive film.

Here are Frida's crutches and iron corset.
The child corpse beside its broken mother.
What conscientious accounts we audit:
paint tubes, nails, ecstasies and tips.
She has learnt from the Inexorable Accountant,
Stalin, prop of steel for a wounded world.
Does she not see: his gigantic head
averted, looking askance at her little one,
has even rationed smiles.
The hand strangles the flying bird.

But here are the two Fridas.
(The one seeking her secret sister
must find the milk store
opening into the interior of the earth.)
An artery runs from the one heart
into the other: the two
have a common circulation system.

What could Diego hope for?

"You, my dear, who are born every hour,
only I can give what you already have."
"I know. And only I can have from you
what you have never had."

It is one and the same heart
but two troubled faces.
The one was here recently,
the other has just come.
(And he who seeks his averted half
must find the trivial door.)

Trotsky drags back the two chairs
he stole in the move.
Not troubled by the dirt.
Requiring history to be retouched
to make the Dream real.

Last is not the popular skeletons,
imprisoned in a kind of mazurka.
Last is the turtle
slowly swimming through the centuries
and yet staying in this room,
beginning to crumble from all it has seen.

7

Death in Alexandria

I saw your discreet depression this morning
in the hotel's experienced mirror:
who rose against you
apart from yourself?
So much older than you, so withered –
I saw it in your hunched shoulders.
Someone seeing herself as your measure.

Down here in the catacombs
where Greek, Egyptian and Roman
quarrel like inseparable drinking companions
(the watchman in toga and dog's head,
the ox with Attic sun between its horns)
we note the blunder of hybrid culture:
on the family tomb the man of stone
steps back into life with his left foot
while the woman desiring to reflect him
thrusts her right foot forward
thus remaining behind in the dark.

Everything by chance means more
than it wishes to mean.
Criticism is greater than poetry,
a misunderstanding as fertile as death itself.
And the flaking mirror-image has,
as opposed to its master, a passport.

The noise of the traffic
is absorbed in the noise of the traffic.
The garbage rummages among the garbage.
And the old man descending from the tram,
a word of Cavafy on his lips,
has paled into his commentary.

This city gives not a damn about living.
This is the city discussing the city:
a constantly expanding section of footnotes

that has reached our rustling lungs
and our paper-thin lips.

Who is approaching me in the lift mirror
with a confidence that is not mine?

Low pressure centred in the Baltic States deepens

Here the road strays out to Sysne Point.
The sea fed forward by the horizon,
perpetually new lines turning
and turning on the same exhausted truths.
The sky ruggedly grey
and so low knees sag. A vein of memory
might have dawdled over the rocks
the scrub momentarily sparkling viper's bugloss.
No memory there.
Behind the pane in the boatswain's low cottage
a glimpse of a hunched old Nietzsche
swearing at the lamp's reeking wick:
it is delaying his final work,
"Tragedy is Dead". The rickety ladder
used by the old village women
to scrub the sky clean in the spring,
lies chopped into wood on the steps.
The tree in the yard is compressed
like the textbook's T-Ford
approaching the speed of light.
No heart is great or foolish.
Even the grass lies low.
Only between the newly-written waves
can you read with a little effort
how history nonetheless insists.

The journey to Thule

We had learnt that you speak kindly to whales. But those
which long followed us with smoky clouds and horrible
screeches made us realise the limits of our language. When
they finally dived, a church wall of water rose that took
our foremast and four crewmen.

But most of all we were terrified by the night that never
was. We made our way ahead in a light jelly which
anticipated the island below the horizon. When the coast at
last appeared, pale and irresolute, we sensed we had long
borne that land within us. Here were no trees, and the
ground was so thin that now in summer the dead could be
perceived – they had already met us out at sea.

Do not misunderstand me. This country has no history.
The eyes of humans are as forgetful and as light as the
night, their handshake ingenuously honest, their thoughts
trustingly scattered along the mountainsides.

The people work for two consecutive days and when they
rest, they lie with their eyes open to watch others working.
They do not like mentioning themselves; the language even
has no word for "I".

Nor can we make out their two sacred watercourses. The
one turns black into white, the other white into black –
upsetting no one.

When we ask how long people have lived there, they find
it difficult to understand our question, preferring to take
up their great export of conscience, the bales on the quays
of stiff sheets dried on the rocks. The people themselves
call their island the Will of God.

Prague quartet

1.

So many listening. Appearing to recognise.
Like the Palace on the hill – a gutted head
filled with suspicions, shelf by shelf.
It is 1985 and shall remain so.
The buildings up there hanging on
though having long lost their foundation.
The cathedral alone has weight and time,
half gust, half stone:
a paralysed ancient
searching for words for his rage.

Here destruction is going on
that senses find hard to grasp
though it is strangely familiar.
As if lashing wingbeats
and tearing claws . . . No, the austere space
denies what one suspects.

"Here nothing but Liberation is going on."

One piece of the past anyhow left:
John of Nepomuk is still hurled into the river
by hands which have not made him voluble.
As if frozen in a fall from the police station window.
Buttercups and carnations heaped by his place
with their archaic plea: "Saue us from Denuntiation."

Wingbeats and claws . . It sounds
as when a culture vanishes.
The scent of lilacs suddenly a phrase
and yet another section inaccessible.

This street was once a piece of Europe.
So many languages, so many ways of thinking
fitting into a pub the size of a hand.

13

The singing from the open window
wants you to recognise –
What is meant by "recognise"?

All the time, these small remnants of flesh
swirling out of nothing –
Glints in the air of black beaks.
The way those crossing the bridges thin out!

We wander in towards the old square,
the walls scraped, dull parchment
struggling against its new text.
Instead of faces, scratches and scars.
The crowd in the square stiffens: a screech of thoughts.
As something trying to be understood.

2.

Slowly the lovers are freed
from the suffocating night,
the hotel room increasingly dissolved.
Like Ascension in the roof of St Nicholas:
they rise through the scarlet smoke
in a stiffening whirl of sheet.
Legs linger a moment
helplessly dangling from the ecstasy
with magnified soles
before the azure takes them, too.
Only the tottering buildings are left,
curved in towards the sudden vacuum.

Stillness. Slowly created
round the waking
timid faces in the plaster:
St Nicholas blessing with fingers splayed
the money-changers in nervous jeans
the master bass-player who lost his post
when he married in the church,
the waitress lugging her country's future –

14

a tray of unwashable porcelain.
Flaking faces, unexpectedly as close
as their own heavy breathing.

3.

Here Kafka is a poltergeist.
Since driven out of the bookshops
he haunts every street in Prague
(which thus becomes a street in Prague).
Told of how Minister M one night
met himself on Charles Bridge.
Still in hospital for what he grasped.
A busload of party men from Bratislava
on a hungry visit to the Ministries
disappeared with an unknown guide. Sometimes
you can hear them inside the walls.
Is that him, the one with an indefinite smile
who hangs a warning notice by Laterna Magika?
(The street beneath the entrance has gone.)
I plod my way through the alien text
and see the theatre audience insisting,
floating in over nerves and veins of the shaft,
Prague's opened thorax:
you browse in a coming year,
discussing its actors.
As if a new production were inevitable
in the inevitably closed theatre

4.

The official spring is condensed
into the concert of the day in St Nicholas.
What wasteful orthodoxy! Trumpets.
The more and more dissolving choir
preaching the People's liberation
from the people. And retaining the year 1985.
Bassoons. Up on the plinth
authority in golden mitre temporarily

15

named St Cyrillus of Alexandria.
Presses the crosier better against the throat
of the heretic here called Nestorian.
Poor thing is bent backwards, bald with pain,
with holes for pupils.
Only the half-open mouth Alive –
his cry halted an inch from the stone.
But why those huge ears?
Do they credit a suffocated dissident
with such tremendous hearing?

Fortissimo: the ceiling slowly opens
for the tornado of faith: the scarlet mist
lifts its people into its realm.

Only a scared bit of sun
offers dissent up in the gallery,
loiters by the organ Mozart played.
That glimpse is enough. Makes clear
what the ears of the heretic are waiting for:
a Beethoven French horn
in one of future's corridors. As uncertain
as when a waking drunk clears his throat.

Dreams. Czesław Miłosz has just declared
the state of Europe is as stable
as after the Congress of Vienna.
But authority wonders with the mitre removed
and for safety's sake is prepared
should the time to change clothes have come.

Up there, perhaps a century away,
is a glimpse of freedom so limitless
that he who is walking across Charles Bridge
risks dispersing like his own breath

The demons are driven out everywhere.
As long as in their eagerness they do not drive
out the bookshop out of the word "bookshop"

and bridges out of the word "bridge".
The crosier is undoubtedly broken that day
the bald heretic free to speak.
But can his words make their way out
better than now if there is no one
worried enough to listen
and scratched enough to recognise?

Questions, questions.
It is surely a hundred years
to the liberation of Liberation.

Scribbled in the margin of history

1.
What we have is but a handful of fragments:
a jawbone of a pre-Socratic,
an odd sarcasm from Versailles
and the lost spurs of the soul of the world.
Out of that we are to create cohesion –
I revert to Hölderlin's idea:
man is an enormous draft.

2.
Yes, I know. I have called the present a country village,
comprehensible only through its place in the empire.
But the word is thrown back bloodied:
"Comprehensible?"
Pedagogics and I have now split up.

3.
To make your way between four and five
can be like trying to put
a jersey on with the sleeves reversed.
Assume the road turns there –

4.
It is no psychic evasive manoeuvre
when so many in Warsaw today
lie low behind safe begonias
in windows of 1939
disowning what has happened since.
It is rather history that recoils.
Subsidence took several decades
and what has happened
cannot happen.

5.
You are deceived by grammar.
"Before" is actually often "after".

As when the master director's latest film
exposes the kitsch in the previous ones,
thus our actions today seem to change
what happened a hundred years ago.

I myself sit here with my grandpa on my lap.
He is furious at the rôle we wish to give him
but is only four months old
and does not extend to language: gg, gg –
His eyes are outside his head.

6.
As if I sought in vain to detach myself
from the faceless darkness
flowing mumbling down the stairs,
floor by floor, century by century:
a darkness we know all too well.

In the hall here within the copper gateway
are piled all thoughts that have been thought.
What a concentrated smell of dust in the dimness!

In the centre are the sarcophagi,
resembling those of the Ming Dynasty
though these are smaller, have lost their colour.
At the third my skin begins to twitch:
I suspect I am by my awaiting grave.
But the guide has read my associations
and shakes his head, explaining
in a voice hoarse with history
that the grave is from what I have just risen.

7.
This is one of history's ambushes.
For a few hours or days
Leningrad has taken back its name.
The policeman leafs through my pocket diary,
going through my memory line by line.
"May I explain, off the record . . ."

20

"There is no off the record here."
His hand sweeps over to the Neva, the starving warehouses,
the hovering palaces, the uniforms
queuing shivering at the ferry.
He is sitting in the answer book.
But leafs on: suspecting I have copied
the line in Marx abolishing Marx.
I look at his hands,
the ring of lead, and recognise
the Mesopotamian temple servant
whose features kept the realm intact.

8.
Sometimes a sudden link can arise
between times unknown to each other.
Then the world grows with a wrench.
The more that meeting resists interpretation
the more indispensable it seems to be.

I distrust the glimmer of explanation.
The source of error is all remnants of God
dispersed in the Creation
but unable to stop working on it –
an absent-minded cancer
giving the illusion of purpose.

A lightning flash between centuries
leaves its black light in the eye.

21

Aśoka's stone

All sounds on board the **Herefordshire**
are too great: the creaking of the hull
claims the world is breaking
and screaming gulls think they are
the unbaptised children of Dante's Inferno.
The hemisphere one long headache
trembling from horizon to horizon.
The glass of port remains untouched,
the rug left on deck.

Only a year or two has passed
since he broke the Brahmin script,
the flickering symbols set
and Aśoka's law appeared in the stone.
But what was intended for a modest article
in the Journal of the Asiatic Society
tore itself free from philology.
The third century before Christ
was suddenly ajar
and a smell of savagery and dust
poured into a drowsy present.

While shaving before the mirror
he saw the barbarians rummaging in drawers
and turned astonished – the room was empty.
And his only son, a few days old
- was to have been named James Prinsep, he too –
had gone: far too fragile a hostage.

But no one walked safely in Calcutta
now the Royal Mint had been infiltrated.
The flapping of tents in the wind
and endless crowds with jingling arms
drew through seemingly deserted streets
demanding 'generosity'.
How thoughtlessly we counted history
among our nourishing colonies.

22

Coastline hardens and Portsmouth is hinted.
One writes winter 1839.
He has perhaps four months left
with the hoofs of the hordes in his head.

Four Greek voices from the earth

1.

I am the loneliest of shadows.
The others shy away from me
as from the stench of a persistent sore.
They don't even let me bear a name
for fear of infection. You think you know
that I am he who showed history the way
and let the Persians attack our forces in the rear
at the pass in whatever it is called.
The others here won't even soil their minds
by knowing my betrayal. No one realises
I was in the service of Necessity,
the divinity forcing the course of events
to an end concealed from us
and demands we turn a deaf ear
when skulls are crushed like shells.
I wished to serve what is greater
than man's loneliness.

2.

Noble is death when bravely you fall in the lead, said the poet.
Nothing noble
in the stab in the back across the shoulderblade
or the thrust at the crotch
of him already fallen to his knees.
Nothing noble either in the women
coming in the night
and ripping from me the fumbling image
of her whom I never cease to love
but search in vain for here
with no image as memory.
Have I wandered for a year or a thousand?
One thing I do know: I am still seeking
the poet who spoke of this wonderful death.
I have saved this little knife,
a rare object down here,
to slice the tongue from his mouth.

3.

Do you know your misunderstanding
is what torments us dead the most?
I am a simple statue, the flat kind,
a woman with arms folded,
a face only just begun,
but I don't lack feelings because of that.
It pains me that you late barbarians
who have exhibited my nakedness
think I served fertility
or showed the way to the ultimate realm.
No, I was lain in the lover's grave
by she who could neither follow him
nor leave him to solitude.
I am the one given kisses of mire
and caresses of naked bone
intended for the living.
Only a heart of stone could cope with that.

4.

Not even the *name* Porphyrius should have survived.
That I still appear among you
is due to the zeal of my enemies.
Just come a little closer.
Not that my voice is diffident
but it has been forced into such detours
words have become as worn as old sandals.
Writings of my own cause have been burnt
by those who thought better
and my thoughts borne away to be racked
by my pious opponents.
What has saved me for posterity
is their need to contradict me –
I reach you through their criticism.
Had they drowned me in the silence of the well,
thrown my books to the swine
and ignored by views

no cunning could have brought me here.
It is their eagerness to silence me
that allows you to hear my voice.

Only do not demand
to see my face.
He who has to make his way
out of crushing argument
and grinding mocking laughter
does not claim much substance.
So you will have to make do with
half a smile here,
a far too experienced wrinkle there.
Between 'neither' and 'nor'
you nonetheless perceive my breath.

Eroica

Of our great archaic epic
remain two odd shards
but they are part of our daily life:

This warrior resting in the brook
water flowing over his face,
obedience loose in the billowing grass.
No thoughts disturb his fragile head,
no compassion in his harrowed breast.
He is gathering strength, biding his time.
His shield is radiating captured sun.

And then this mad king
we again found in his scorched forest
and had to haul back to his peacock throne.
We bound him lovingly to the back
with straps still rendolent of cattle.
He regards himself as defeated, and dead.
But we don't seem to comply.

Conquest of the future

Through tears of pride
we see the caravels lift
and retreat through space with bellying sail,
furrows of sea-fire behind.
They already escape the human eye
but occasionally obscure a star
and each time distress me.
As if our jubilation held a core of tears.

Our fleet is to conquer 2060
once the previous year is scraped clean.
The fruit of halcyon peace prevails
since the future was divided
– along the equator of faith –
between the squabbling princely houses.
D'Este await instructions shortly
on size of mining and number of slaves.
The future faces are no doubt too thin
to be seen in damp-spotted report
but the number should reach us: may it suffice
to pay for the year's consumption.

Not the slightest resistance heard.
The greenery is safely changed for gold,
the atmosphere for lead right there
to ease the transport home.
And I have my pox-mark behind my ear
against intertemporal infection.

Am probably entitled to confidence
while in my binoculars I see
the convoy's sparkling wash extinguished.

To Homero Aridjis

28

IV

Epistle

I am writing to you from a distant country –
that's how the strongest letters start.
But I know nothing of distance.
I am writing to you from a country so close
it cannot be surveyed.
Here are towns so close
our senses cannot grasp them;
crowds in the streets and window lights
evidently harsh and immediate
as stench and glint of old fish box
but on this side of focus.
Piles of cuttings around me in vain
try to make the present visible.
I fumble in the flood of time and meanings
and grasp a glitter with no substance.
Astonished, I embrace the one I love
and her face is so close
neither of us has a name.
We miss the life we live!

I am writing to you from the country that is
but can be made out only in a hundred years
when she and I have been erased
only the empty names remaining.

In my beginning is my end

1.
It is the harsh Glimminge house
one endless evening of autumn and crows.
A Rosencrantz, the family sly artist
with a query in place of year of death,
takes stock of his cooling work:
the bottle with a Bacchant in enamel.

That same evening, some century later,
in an equally dexterous way
he takes the pretty maid to bed
and paints in her pudenda
the features of a bucolic Michelangelo,
condemned to suffocate in dung and envy –

(The bastard name Roos has just stopped his son
carving an Assyrian lion
out of the hard darkness behind him.)

But the seed goes impatiently on.

While I write
the old enamel master sticks
his still randy hand into my head
and from inside, fingers my stern eye.
Seems temporarily content but just as restless.
What does he want in me?

2.
This is Espnäs. A poorly illuminated inn
has been waiting here a century
for more preachers and surveyors.
What barren forests, north of north.
What chill also in the urn with father
we have just lowered into the disobliging mumbling
in Strömsund's restrained churchyard:
the country boy who went out into the world

30

to become a handful of irresolute ash
among steps and rustle of fencing posts
constantly being moved down there.

I suppose we never met.
Our phrases together seeking,
fly-rods swinging in unhappy expectation,
ripples testing out an alien prow:
a clumsy chapter with a whiff of petrol.

But also through an untrained father
the seething voices may arrive:
an inn beneath the earth
with doors swinging in the lower wind
and guests unwilling to give their names.

In that village by the lake
a separation changed Creation.
Someone stole the sky-globe itself
misappropriating both shores.
Explain then to a four year old
that unfortunately he is ruined.
And shall not touch on the word 'home'.
A draft contained on a faded postcard
on which the stamp portrays a falling king.

I still live in a draft –
have wasted not a minute on the question
"Who am I?" Cope with the mirror in my lodging
in precisely the many seconds
it takes to knot my black tie.

Doors of ash swing in the draught.
Guests of ash come and go.
Northern lights that night: moving inexorably
to and fro, with no explanation.

I am afraid you misunderstood me.
This is not about a transmigration.
My discarded worries
are the compulsion to live all my lives
in this present, this ill-fitting epoch itself,
with no time even to think about the matter.
In a hiatus at the theatre last night
an unknown ancient nodded to me
right across the chasm
as a father makes himself known.
And at a wind-ruined halt this morning
a strange girl took my hand,
saying I had forgotten her pocket-money.
But my really sweaty problem
is to cope with my four full-time jobs
without the management noticing
and to keep my wives apart –
none of them would forgive.
I half-run all the time, in my sleep, too.

Sagging from the weight of all the keys.
What anguish suddenly comes to me
from one of my hidden lives.

Naturally you recognise yourself.
Why then this surprise and anger
in your four faces?

Siesta in Lesbos

It glints as if sea between the trees:
my first ever glimpse of time –
wave after wave after wave,
a ceaseless wandering to the shore
though not one wave leaves its place.

After lunch of grapes, sheep's cheese and wine,
you sleep with your head in my lap.
Your dreams flow out between the trees
like blood in water.
And I am appalled by their sternness:
image after image in which I struggle across the world
but am always left in the same place,
that of suffering.
As if I had sold my soul to the shadows.
The reproach of the dream hurts
but half my heart agrees.
What was the messenger doing in defeat?

Is it not the chronicler
who gives the dreadful war its form?
And the archaeologist interpreting a smashed skull,
is he not akin to the man with the axe?

Wave after wave after wave between the trees,
a wandering that goes nowhere.
I struggle to where I already am
and call it responsibility.
The glint out there is dazzling,
is going out and dazzling.
Then you wake
and the last line is never written.

Vallis Clausa

Here is path in path in place of grass.
The waterfall worn out
and greenery photographed away.

Turned away from the tourists
Petrarch stands out in the water
his cap pulled down against the light.
The closed valley round him persists
with the force of *her* smile.
He stands in the inordinate greenery,
he stands in the cool and the blackbird's song
at the very boundary of perception.

As close as skin next to skin
when nightjar has ceased and moon paled
the other life loiters:
the life I did not choose.
As if after a fork in the road
you took only one way
and not both at once.
Steps along the other way
along the side of the closed valley
are noted in a pain with no address.

The greenery closes round the figure
you thought you had excluded.
With water rippling round his knees
he stands in the other life.

Impromptu

It is a wild wind-ruined day.
We have quarrelled, blackening plaster on the wall
but found a way back
to you, to me.
I rise a little so the sweaty
skin drops rustling from my skin
and I settle my heart right in yours;
a clay plate upturned into another.

The window is open: May is blue.
In the beam above us death
advances a thousandth of an inch, with a click.
But the rosefinch on the bare branch
sings, sings,
the down on his breast turning in the wind.
How much greater is the song
than the quaking body.

Written in stone

Come closer, even closer,
so close that you can touch the text.
I grope towards you from within the stone.
If you press your fingertips to mine
you can feel the pulse from a world
that hung together as if a conspiracy.
I myself remember nothing of my life
but think I wrote my way towards a greater self
who was to live in my words,
door open to anyone who cared.

Perhaps I was country boy from the start.
If you lean your brow against the stone
you will doubtless hear my sturdy thoughts
as a distant ox-cart along the mountain road.
Possibly I became a kind of orator
and took the crowd along in a murmur
easy to mistake for life.

Come closer, a millimetre into the stone.
Lend me your voice
and I shall tell you who you are.
Lend me your eyes
and I shall show you a world
which one minute makes the world distinct.
Lend me your breath
and with a gasp you shall understand
that you have lived for very long.

V

Silent apocalypse

Out of oblivion and indifference
the four come riding,
so worn by centuries of reproductions
their weary features
can be taken as creases in the paper.
Their hoofs so light the dew untouched,
their howls discreet as a young swallow's snore.

The first swings a scourge of straw
and the green of the jungle turns white.
The second thrusts his stave into the river
and fish come floating belly up.
The third shoots a flintarrow into space
and alien light falls in through the wound –
bewildered you see the arm turn speckled.
The fourth strews the houses from his sack
and the multitude couple, blind as flies,
in order again and again to fill the earth.

The four now thunder down the street,
silent as a cloud of dust. Our late language
can scarcely see or smell them.
Only sleep has words
for what we have long expected
but have no courage to recognise.
The sleeping make a gesture
as if to praise, or defend themselves
and imperceptibly cease to breathe.

Tulum

Nervous temples. Breakers, breakers.
The open place seems to be listening
like a parabola antenna to space.
And we are obviously a disturbance.

Three brown pelicans
draw an experienced slice across the coast
accentuating our chance circumstance.

As if shadows of fingers had examined my face.
The dead realm explores
the realm that thinks it is alive.
Someone reads the visitor's hand
and is horrified by betrayal and greed,
feeling already on our breath
that we have broken the cycle between
animals, air and water, man,
placing ourselves outside Creation.

At all cost, *we* must be hindered
making our way into the days of the Maya:
with trembling hands, the astronomer calculates
the lifespan of our culture
with a seven minute margin of error,
breathing freely over the result.

Now we also hear the heavens tightening.
As if the god would soon be descending
in a tempest of feathers
and we annihilated by his gaze.

In the empty waterhole
it gleams of sudden water
and small fish that have long kept it fresh.

But nothing happens.
And I realise the visit of the god

is not located in time:
occurring never and incessantly
beyond reach of the senses
in which he ravages on.

The visit

This is a village in Michoacan.
High moon, squat shadows,
the world bordered by calm mountains.
Two thousand people are asleep:
not even in their soundest sleep
have they witnessed riches.

Then from an unknown dimension
come trucks and fierce bulldozers,
the wheels as silent as wings of moth,
men's features as anonymous as the moon's.
In the silenced hour
they dig a place for a lake
and heave into it their viscous past:
acids as nervous as liberated snakes,
crimes glistening straight through the barrels,
contracts the fire declined to touch.

Before the moon is down, the visitors are gone.

In chilly morning the villagers go out
and rub their eyes
at signs of visit from above:
shattered trees, glistening tracks in the grass.
They salvage the magnificent barrels
glowing green-blue with divinity
to store their drinking water in.

Chichén Itzá

This Monday is the chink: my opportunity
to come here for the first time.

This is where the observatory is
stars and destinies can be kept in check.
This is also where you can glimpse,
just before the snake casts its shadow,
the dead world taking place in the living.

Politicians stride in Miami shorts
from pyramid to the house of warriors
and clap their hands: creating echoes
to plot the point
where history awaits them.

If you whisper at one end of the pitch
you may be heard five centuries away.
Anyone with the strength to listen
can also sense the dark, creative
half of his own childhood.
(I hear two women in rustling petticoats
shuffling round their despair:
a cupboard they never get right in the room.)

But the purpose of the pitch is the Game.
The burning globe bouncing
from one leather-clad underarm
to another's head, a third's chest,
must never touch the ground.
Then the cosmos is disturbed.
And the one whose hands touch the sun
is turned to ash and shame.
The goal is an eye of stone
permitting only the best to compete,
only the best to look on:
financiers, pop stars, junta generals
and the occasional artist craftsman

from the epoch of uncertainty.
The winner has the honour of his head
being liberated from his unclean body
and raised on a pole to speak with the gods.

The row of triumphant skulls
slowly turns into wind-tortured stone,
a mumbling frieze
as endless as the silence of the gods.

In front of the expanding museum
we are met by black hairless dogs
(favoured in the days of Aztecs
but nowadays extinct).
They examine us carefully with running eyes
that are eight centuries old.
They cannot bark, have never needed to.
Their mission is to wait us out.
Just now they appear to be guarding
the house with Diego Rivera's visions.

Not until half an hour later
faced with small terracotta figures
from the slow days before Columbus
does it dawn on me
the dogs actually bear human masks.

Outside the calendar

Sian Ka´an is Maya
for the place where heaven is born.
Now the vault is a few hours old
but already larger than I have seen it:
a blue used for the first time.

The boat is poled closer to the isle.
What is it making my watch go slow
and the dollar in my pocket into waste paper?
They are there! What archaic clapper-bills.
Half foliage,
the flock of spoonbill broods
on the days we fear and at the same time
hope for with our averted half.

Then one of their species descends
out of the blue depths
legs outstretched towards the nest,
its huge pink wings flapping
and your heart slows its beats.
Lower and lower it sinks
with outspread stilled plumage.
Lower and lower it sinks.
Your tongue is then rough crust in your mouth.
I realise this is the point
where time can no longer be imagined.

VI

Illuminations

In Lau, I stood before the peasant cathedral,
opened the door a finger's width,
prepared for the white cool inside
and was turned to stone. Perhaps it was acoustics
and voices of the attenders together with the gap –
I have no need for an explanation.
But the whole church was a tremendous mouth
turbulent with voices of the angels.
No mercy found in that music.

2.
The children sit beside each other
singularly white
in a white room before a white piano.
It is our dining-room yet not.
Their hair is so fair,
your eye shies.
They laugh when bass and descant
are in unforeseen agreement.
The music also seems white.
The children may be fifteen and twelve;
hard to decide
as they weigh nothing
and the image refutes a context.
Something is wrong with the daylight.
It is far too light,
also for those high windows.
Then you can see the white wallpaper
darkening at the edge, curling
and letting through a flame, more and more.

3.
With the handle of my dripping umbrella
I knock on the sarcophagus
and urge you out
of the third row
in the Escorial below.

Silence, the rain raging up there.

Realise you are expecting me
in your royal study.
The stairs wind through the years,
thunder collecting itself for the visit.

4.
In the middle of life, this wallpaper door
must always have been here
though we never noticed it.
I open it
– it sounds like tearing a sheet –
and the smell of cancelled years moulders out.
Behind it sits a withered woman
in a chamber smaller than a wardrobe,
her eyes beyond all conversation,
the figure blurred by cobwebs.
The wrinkled lips are whispering
white with anger:
Could you not have let me die!

5.
I sit shaving on the steps.
The maple screening off the road and the world
is a noisy Russian novel
containing the whole history of the farm.
In today's section something is at stake.

Shave off a drift of lather and stubble:
there is no face inside.
I shall have to live with that
as with the lack of linguistic link
with the swallow swooping in under the eaves:
a jet plane landing in a carwash
but not agreeing with a metaphor.

It is early, before the text,
birches illuminated through.

It is so light, the green in the grass gives up.
"Only if you give up your name
may you step out into the landscape."

The wild chervil drifts, a possible rescue.
"You have a few minutes to go."
The rabbit in the grass is still
its throat throbbing:
it declines all interviews.

6.
This is before the gladiator game
and we are still back in the Forum.
The column of Jewish captives
in Titus' triumphant arc
trembling and humming is a swarm of bees
clinging on in an intermediate landing.
But what has captivated me
is the piece of capital on the ground:
its chiselled acanthus leaf
breaking out of the stone and verdant.
In the slightly spicy scent I stand
reading script that was never written.

7.
No one relates unpunished
the Emperor's secret army in Xián.
A shattered warrior comes to see me
in the company of my kinsman Bei Dao.
His voice cracked, mind cracked
and cracked clay crashing round him
but he comes towards me with dignity
and signals with his grey hand
that I am summoned to the Emperor's realm.
As if he had not brought that realm with him!
Cracks run across sky and streets.
My friends round me
speak of our crackled days,
clay dust running from mouth corners.

A crack runs right across the mirror.
Impossible to see if it is in the glass
or in my claygrey eye.

8.
I seem to have been washed overboard.
Between two cold gulps
I see the ship retreating between clouds,
a sensuality I have never noticed before:
the moist gleam in the stern windows
and the pregnant calm of the sails.
While the ship grows smaller and smaller
its contours become more and more clear.
I realise: it is heading for the needle's eye.

I myself am left in a ground swell of darkness.
What I feel is no terror
but a grief so great
it dissolves my limbs.

9.
I have gone out to fetch wood
but am halted here
in front of the south window.
As I am in darkness
you cannot see me in there.
The last of the fire glows in the stove
I made with these hands
(nor can they be seen
in a night with no stars).
The children are both small and grown,
captivated by a game like Mah Jong
but with frightening stakes.
Your face stares steadily
out towards the dark: an expectation
expecting nothing.
What is it that stops me
giving one single little sign?

VII

To Gerard

We were speaking of art
but were interrupted
before we came to the knotty rôle of Patron.

How do you intervene
without intervening
when the paint hesitates before the canvas?
You were gone with the answer.

But I know you will soon pass again
at the level of the window,
slipping lightly among the flakes of space
on your way home
the picture carefully pressed to your chest.
Almost a year younger.

Gods of Gotland

Autumn makes no attempt at sky,
only streaks of mist and floating cows.
The sudden chill assures the cyclists:
That's all there is.
No high or low.
This is a Greece flattened out
by the values of ultimate time.

So the gods live discreetly:
can crunch on the gravelly road,
glow dully in frost-bitten cynanchum
or shimmer like phosphorous in the fur
of a run-over rabbit.

They once flowed here like driftwood
forcing the island to rise from the water.

Terra amata

So untroubled
the skull in the museum case
beyond thousands of centuries of blistered glass.
Staring at what we call Baie des Anges.
He lived before all war
therefore is hard to understand.
Darkness in the eyes: all that he sees
darkness from his mouth: all he wants to say.
But swift reflexes alternate round the crown:
the glitter of water across the same bay
as the one I think I can see.

His days can be reconstructed here and there:
the hut and hearth, the evening's feast
on the elephant they together succeeded in felling.
But what does he know of the world?
I tap on the pane
with village schoolmaster's inquisitive finger.

I should never have reached out my hand.
The landslide was imperceptible,
its effect clear. It is suddenly uncertain
what is before and what after.
He knows nothing of his withered mind
or the holes of darkness of his eyes.
He has just leapt out of his morning:
the rain sweeping over the bay,
the scent of thyme tightening the nose –
but stronger still is the smell of danger.
He has just caught sight of me.
As if he had dug for roots in his dream
and brought up my lecturing skull.
Nothing in his eyes
of the archaeologist's grief
at days so hopelessly out of reach.
He sees the days I cannot see
because I am inside them.

51

And his eyes are large, black with distaste,
a seething troubled life
round his raucous cry of warning.

Journey to Jämshög

The railbus hurtles through a tunnel
of hastily sketched spring,
the sun glimpses newborn and red
in indecisive mist.
Only the thump from the rail-joints
indicates the existence of time.
The semaphore at a halt
signals a yellow "I'll come too!"
but is not taken seriously.
It will be a long time before man
may be included on the journey.

Water now glints in the mist,
wood anemone created: a sudden meadow.
Beeches leave a still pale green
contribution to a new attempt.

The time has come. The approximation that is me
descends at Jämshög with his case
and the lecture: only an outline of life.
In front of the red station building
among flapping pigeons from the new world
is Harry Martinson, thinner than I remember,
in collarless shirt and shivering,
hands thrust into trouser pockets.
He examines me as if I were alive.
Not until after several breaths do I see
he is the natural superintendent
in this new existence.
He sees my confusion
and grins as broadly
as when he has told us a good yarn.

The unwritten poems

This is another Calcutta.
The people here, on the bed, on the floor,
in the window niches, forming a listening pattern
with Mahasveta Devi in the middle.
In the undecided room next door,
women clatter with buckets: a big wash
looking askance at her thoughts.
The narrow red stairs leading up here
are a swirl of iron: to remember life, she says
with a smile that takes her words back.

Half her life
is in her work on shelves,
the other half in these files
stacked on table and floor.
Voices and chink of spade on stone
emerge from between the pages.
Here are her collected unwritten poems.

Thirty years she has wandered between villages,
in jungle country of the elephants.
She hears the huts crying: "We have no water!"
She hears the swarm of children wanting to be a school
and the felled forest that hopes:
"Can you get money for plants
that help us to remember life?"

She writes to all authorities
in charge of the four elements.
Gives voice to anguish of unknown tribes,
symbols to language that has no script.
As she writes a prayer for electricity
villagers stand round her
with fifteen watt faces.

Those who mourn the dead come here,
sit silently around her,

the mumble in an outer circle continuing
from files mourning the living:
We have no rain. Our children are drying up.
What do we do with a life that is no life?

She sits in the difficult middle
writing each and every one of them
with his own trembling hand.

Route tournante

Cézanne has placed a surly easel
in what is still not there.
He feels the geology of absence,
layer upon layer, so well that even bare
fields of canvas are quite authentic.

The road that turns in last year's grass
is still just a bend in the mind,
stolen from an old Chinese.
It begins in a soiled chapter
he has scraped away with his knife –
you were never there

Begin with the shadows
and work towards the lightening middle.
The blue-grey may tempt back a field.

Like his life this treacherous year:
the throbbing foot that will not heal
contemplates deserting him.
While the road insists anew –
what thirst for sun!

Among women in dark headcloths,
his mother, bowed in the grief of the dead.
As the others vanish beyond the bend
she makes excuses to stay,
like a misty blue on the road.

How hard to endure another's touch –

It is the colour that may touch the world.
Naturally he has mentioned the logic. And the cone.
But those are approximate values.
No theory can take hold of
the raging forces inside things.

Only a grasp of colours
can force 'reality' to an answer.

Patch upon patch, a stubborn gamut,
extracting a village from the village:
gables, church tower, a possible road
and a fugue of swallows.
Every house is uninhabited: waiting
for whoever can make his way back.

A day is a year.

Like his life –
took decades to see that verdure is blue.
And now he has succeeded in a few minutes
in painting the sound of bells.

The paintbrush lowers.
The canvas has forced out a landscape
in what only calls itself landscape.
And the road really does turn.
Every second has a moist gleam
none could see before.
He stands with his throbbing ache
in suddenly fresh last year's grass.

Note

Some poems in this collection revert to motifs recognisable from previous books, so 'Illuminations 2' again takes up the prelude to 'The Children in the White Room' in **The Secret Meal**. Here is the original "illuminated" version – before the master builder and the pedagogue intrude.

Perhaps it should also be mentioned that Petrarch's Vallis clausa ('The Closed Valley') is today's Fontaine-de-Vaucluse and that Terra amata is a museum in Nice containing the remnants of the oldest known settlements in Europe. It should perhaps also be added that Gerard Bonnier (1917–1987) was a leading Swedish publisher, art collector and patron of the arts, and that Jämshög is the author Harry Martinson's childhood village (now the seat of an association in his memory). Otherwise, unusual people or places – from the patron saint of Bohemia, John of Nepomuk, to the Maya cult places Tulum and Chichén Itzá – are probably defined by their context.

The following are some general comments extracted from a huge number of extensive reviews from Swedish daily papers in October, 1992:

. . . Kjell Espmark is a demanding poet: his refusal to accept every variant of recommended optimism or belief in the future never leads to a position of crustiness or escapism. He is more like a social observer, methodically establishing that no one escapes, that the victims are you and me, the state and the market, communism and capitalism, on a macro- and micro-level. The patterns of Society choose us and swallow us.
. . . Many would no doubt put the epithet pessimism on Espmark. I find him the opposite, factual, stern, truthful. Black and white, good and evil etc. can never become such a richly orchestrated opposing pair of poems. The suite *Prague*

Quartet should be reproduced and read all over Europe . . . Few poets have such a good and apparently uncomplicated relationship to the actual art . . . in one way Espmark is immediately accessible, a flow of water. But the flow is deceptive . . . under any circumstances, whenever the road turns, 'Route tournante' is a collection of poems you return to. (Jan Karlsson: *Bohustidningen*)

. . . Kjell Espmark is least of all a navel-contemplating poet. He is filled with history, with the cultural heritage of Europe, with the politics of today and, last but not least, all those individual voices he seems to hear rising from tombs and old manuscripts. He is unusual in that he is a poet of both history and our own family, a collective poet, one could say. Anyhow, unusual he is – and has been our very best poet for over fifteen years. (Tommy Olofsson: *Svenska Dagbladet*)

. . . But we meet a poet equally travelled in history as in geography, two dimensions that come together naturally. His camera eye catches the world of today, swiftly superimposed on to that of yesterday. (Björn Nilsson: *Expressen*)

. . . My somewhat late meeting with Kjell Espmark's poetry not only made me change my mind but also became a reading experience. It is not always easy to fix the content of his poems, so freely do they move in time and space . . . it is easy to be carried along by them – by the disciplined and suggestive imagery, but also by an epic energy which drives and bears the poems with it. (Leif Nylén: *Dagens Nyheter*)

. . . He is a reflective poet . . . who has more and more come to meditate on the fleetingness of life and our own ephemeral rôle on earth. (Ulf Wittrock: *Upsala Nya Tdning*)

. . . makes him into one of the foremost of the nation's living poets today. His seriousness, the all-embracing perspective and formal linguistic use of language is something that guarantees an evaluation of that kind. (Bo Jonsson: *Borås Tidning*)

. . . This is a great collection in many ways and emphasises the continuity of Kjell Espmark's writing from his first volume in 1956. . . . He is also one of our most interesting poets, headstrong perhaps, but always open to us as readers, and purposefully ensuring that his allusions shall be kept comprehensible and accessible. . . . 'Route tournante' is quite simply a book of poems which takes us round the world together with a constantly shifting poet-self . . . But his poetry has the fresh immediacy that signifies all great poetry. (Ulf Jönsson: *Gefle Dagbladet*)

. . . Kjell Espmark is the architect among Swedish poets. There has always been a perceptible design beneath his texts and his books are carefully composed. . . . The result has become more colourful than before, but the poet's voice is nonetheless perfectly recognisable – it is not only the art of building in this writer. Here remains the fragmented world and bitter criticism of today. Awareness of history is strong and painful. . . . (Magnus Ringgren: *Aftonbladet*)

. . . 'Route tournante' is rich and an adventure in empathy and intellect. (Sten-Ove Bergwall: *Dala Demokraten*)

. . . (the title poem) I remember and become younger, that is the vision. Memory is stronger than death. The poem, trembling with all its enclosed pain and longing to gather history into the present, arouses the senses and celebrates in visions and confirmations . . . (Tomas Löthman: *Ljusna Bollnäs*)

. . . Almost surprisingly, here is a personal almost private note, unusual in most of Espmark's writing: he has preferred to look into his surroundings, the society we live in, rather than turn inwards, examining the truth about and in his own spiritual life. . . . Here the road turns back into the secret caves where poetry echoes . . . (Curt Bladh: *Sundsvalls Tidning*)

. . . Kjell Espmark writes coolly, but never tepidly, which is why the lack of temperament is fully compensated by his unswerving truthfulness. (Ragnar Strömberg: *Göteborgs-Posten*)

. . . To seek out places and people who have been forced into silence, to give them once again a voice: that seems to run right through Kjell Espmarks lyrical work. In a geographically, culturally and historically expanding movement, like an acute traveller, he is carried from the twilight land of Sweden to more and more distant climes with that aim in mind. (Jesper Olsson: *Östgöta Correspondent.*)

Other Scandinavian Titles Published by Forest Books

Preparations for Flight & Other Swedish Stories
Translated by Robin Fulton

Robin Fulton, one of the best-known translators of contemporary Swedish literature, has gathered a collection of stories which, as he says in his preface, remained in his mind long after a first reading. In all of them, concrete reality evokes mystery, and in many of them, childhood reflections affect and are affected by everyday adult experience.

ISBN 0 948259 66 3   paper £8.95   176pp

Spring Tide
by Pia Tafdrup
Translated from the Danish by Anne Born

Spring Tide is a book about desire, about woman's passion. From inception through total immersion in sensual emotion towards an apprehension of winter's cold, Pia Tafdrup links personal ecstasy with the cyclic rhythm of life. Hailed by Scandinavian critics as a young Danish poet of exceptional talent, Pia Tafdrup, in this sustained sequence of thought–provoking poems, turns language into experience.

ISBN 0 948259 55 8   paper £6.95   96pp

Snow and Summers
by Solveig von Schoultz
Translated from the Swedish by Anne Born

Snow and Summers presents the cream of von Schoultz's poetry from almost fifty years for the first time in English. 'For both poet and reader', writes Bo Carpelan, 'von Schoultz's poetry is an exercise in the sharpening of vision . . .

sincerity and smiling wisdom engendered by a lifetime of experience.'

ISBN 0 948259 52 3   paper £7.95   128pp

Heartwork
by Solveig von Schoultz
Translated from the Swedish
by Marlaine Delargy & Joan Tate

Winner of numerous literary prizes, Solveig von Schoultz is widely acknowledged as one of Finland's leading poets and prose writers. 'Her short stories', writes Bo Carpelan, 'present an acute and subtle analysis of human relationships – between adults and children, men and women, and between different generations . . . She is not only a listener and an observer: she is also passionately involved with these dramas of everyday life which are all concerned with the problems of human value and human growth. These she portrays without sentimentality but with the rich perception of experience.'

ISBN 0 948259 50 7   paper £7.95   144pp

Eyes from a Dream
Poems by Agneta Pleijel
Translated by Anne Born
Introduced by Ruth Fainlight

Agenta Pleijel lived in Poland during the first, abortive attempt by Solidarity in 1981 to free the Polish nation from tyranny. In her 'Polish Suite', translated here for the first time into English, she records the excitement and the fear of living through these months, when 'everything seemed possible' and a whole nation struggled to 'rise from the stones'. But Pleijel is also a Swede, and her 'Winter in Stockholm', in which she comes to terms with a painful childhood, is a timely reminder that freedom too is not without those things that test the courage of the individual to the limits.

ISBN 1 85610 015 4   paper £6.95   64pp

Enchanting Beasts
An Anthology of Modern Women Poets in Finland
Edited and translated by Kirsti Simonsuuri

This anthology of eleven women poets brings the reader some of the best modern poetry from Finland. High lyrical intensity, brave honesty about the human condition, and particularly about the female experience, wit, and a feeling for nature are characteristics shared by all these poets writing in the northernmost corner of Europe, in a landscape of strong contrasts, of light and darkness.

ISBN 0 948259 68 X   paper £8.95   144pp

Hour of the Lynx
A play by Per Olov Enquist
Translated by Ross Shideler

A young boy is committed to a psychiatric institution for a motiveless murder. A sensitive and challenging play, *The Hour of the Lynx* focuses on the boy's role in a controlled experiment in which the researcher gives him a cat to care for. The pastor and the researcher struggle to understand the boy's complex emotional riddles which ultimately reveal profound insights into the mystery and miracle of love and salvation. Enquist is one of Scandinavia's foremost dramatists; productions of his work in Scandinavian and European theatres have established him as a leading European writer.

ISBN 0 948259 85 X   paper £6.95   64pp

The Seer and Other Norwegian Stories
by Jonas Lie
Translated by Brian Morton & Richard Trevor

Trolls or unconscious impulses? Jonas Lie, Norway's great nineteenth century writer, had by his own admission, a twilight nature. Like the landscape, it shifted from light to dark in a fantastic world of superstition. *The Seer* and eight other shorter stories reveal the progress over a period of time towards that darkening vision – towards the belief that within each one of us there is a small, exciting and incalculable troll.

ISBN 0 948259 65 5   paper £8.95   160pp

Room Without Walls
Selected poems of Bo Carpelan
Translated from the Swedish by Anne Born

Perhaps the greatest poet writing in Finland today, Bo Carpelan takes much of his inspiration from the landscape of Finland, its stern northern wintry presence and its delicate spring and summer. In style concise, pure and clear, in form economical, he writes with a delicate lyrical beauty of fundamental human experience. Beneath the spare, deceptively simple surface lie vast eternities, gentle echoes, mysteries, sorrows, signs and warnings.

ISBN 0 948259 08 6   paper £7.95   144p illustrated

The Naked Machine
Poems by Matthias Johannessen
Translated by Marshall Brement

This is the first volume of a contemporary Icelandic poet to be published in England. Already translated into many languages, Matthias Johannessen is acknowledged as one of Iceland's greatest living poets. The translator, Marshall Brement, is also a poet and met Johannessen while American Ambassador to Iceland.

ISBN 0 948259 43 4   paper £5.95   96pp illustrated
ISBN 0 948259 44 2   cloth £7.95   96pp illustrated